Psychological Happiness 'How To Get Thought Control'

By
Paul Wilkins

Introduction

How you feel is influenced by a combination of external and internal influences.

While you have little control over what is going on in the world and the external influences it has on life, Paul explains how to turn the thoughts you have into something like a shield to protect yourself from seeing the negativity and how to make your own feelings become more positive.

Paul also shows how to transform negative influences into something positive, or if this is not possible then put to the back of the mind and left dormant or forgotten, and every one of us can control the thoughts in our mind for this to happen - it is just knowing how to.

Reading this should teach you how to feel more relaxed with life in general, and this is definitely beneficial when there are lots of negativities around as they will mostly pass by.

Contents

1. An Introduction To Therapeutic Poetry

Here's some therapeutic poetry for you
Which has helped out quite a few
A short number of poems covering 'Happiness and Joy'
That everyone should enjoy

The most therapeutic one I'd recommend you reading if you deeply need cheering up being the 'Love, Joy and Delight' one. This is the first poem I ever did though still the best and most enjoyable one lots of people favour.

Each of these poems has a nice rhyme
So you could also have the medicine of laughter some of the time
I've always had a G.S.O.H.
And that's not just a rumour

As a final message and introduction from me called Paul I hope you each enjoy them all.

    i.   Love, Joy & Delight

    ii.   Smile & The World Smiles With you

    iii. Success

    iv. Valued Friendship

    v.   The Power Of Love

    vi. Astrological Horoscopes

    vii. Avoid Any Loneliness & Isolation

    viii. Be Happy Forever, Sad Hardly Ever Again

    ix. How are people thinking healthwise

If you'd also enjoy a few witty jokes, time to time, feel free to view the 'You Must Be Joking' section of my website www.poetryemotion.org.uk

i.   Love, Joy & Delight

Your mind and emotion hold the key
They're the things to set you free
What 'er the day
What 'er the night
Fulfil yourself with love, joy & delight

Sadness and worry
Gets you nowhere at all
Just up the wall
What 'er the day
What 'er the night
Fulfil yourself with love, joy & delight

With faith in the Lord
And determination
You may live a long and happy life
What 'er the day
What 'er the night
Fulfil yourself with love, joy & delight

Let people come first where 'er you go
That's a thought
All people should show
What 'er the day
What 'er the night
Fulfil yourself with love, joy & delight

Love, joy & delight
Love, joy & delight

© Paul Wilkins 1993

ii.   Smile And The World Smiles With You

Everyone should have a warm heart
And in having love for one another play a part
Be very pleasant and polite
Through each day and night

We need to all give each other a grin
And a very happy life begin
The more love and joy you give
The higher with it you do live

Happiness is also a key to good health
Which is worth much more than wealth
Joy is something wanted by very many
That doesn't cost a penny

Entirely everyone in life does achieve a great lot
Though think positively of it they do not
But if you think 'I AM VERY HAPPY' as your endeavour
Alone, and with others, you'll smile forever

© Paul Wilkins 21/08/04

iii.   Success

I've gone from weakness to strength
At a great length
Climbed many a mountain
Watching my troubles fall from the fountain
And I'm going to continue to succeed
No matter how hard a deed

© Paul Wilkins 25/07/04

iv. Valued Friendship

I'm a good leader and organiser without a single doubt
And for plenty a friend often sorting different things out
I'm also an all round creative writer
Who's each day getting brighter

I often give my friends the medicine of laughter
With jokes that are sometimes getting dafter
Because I have a G.S.O.H.
And that's not just a rumour

In the summer hip hip hurray
We can together have a nice holiday
And whilst having a friendly talk
Go for a countryside walk

Then just like we ought
We can play a bit of sport
And for the shuttlecock giving a shout
Have each other running about

Together playing badminton
Me and my friends have quite a bit of fun
We can then have a meal, drink and chat
Whilst trying to not again get too fat

Going through many different life stages
Me and John have known each other for ages
And both covered oh quite a distance
To one another come of great big assistance

© Paul Wilkins 11/02/2020

v.   The Power Of Love

We should all be loving and caring
And warm heart sharing
Bringing to this world love joy and delight
Through each day and night
With the power of love
From heaven above

© Paul Wilkins 11/02/2020

6

vi.   Astrological Horoscopes

If you are called a Capricorn
As a very clever person you are born
Whilst those who are an Aquarius
Often do things that are quite hilarious

When it comes to the Pisces
They all love sailing the seven seas
And most of the Aries
Have a nice big belief in fairies

With those who are a Taurus
Very good at singing in a chorus
People that are born a Gemini
Often watch time fly by

Each person who is a Cancer
Is usually a very good dancer
With a Leo what's most appliant
Is them each being very reliant

Those who are a Virgo
Have a lot of talent to show
Each human that's a Libra
Is always trying to just kid ya

With plenty a Scorpio
Lots of all round good things they do know
Lastly with people born a Sagittarius
The food they most enjoy is quite various

© Paul Wilkins 04/08/13

7

vii. Avoid any Loneliness and Isolation

When it comes to helping people avoid isolation
Lots of health centres and charities can assist with no hesitation
With not a bit of surprise
They help lots and lots of people socialize

If you want to get out and about with friendly people today
You should look at 'meet-up' clubs on your laptop with no delay
Because there's plenty of social events arranged by them to be found
To help everyone with happiness and nice company get around

In each area of the UK there's advertised many a 'meet-up' club
Together going walking, followed by a meal and drink at the pub
Giving everybody a chance to have a quite friendly conversation
And no longer face any isolation

So please never feel stuck on your own
When you can join a 'meet-up' club via a computer or by using your phone
You can get to know of everywhere by contacting your local 'Citizen Advice'
Who could come of assistance for a very cheap price

Also if after going out and about, when at home
You once more feel alone
With no doubt you should ring 'The Samaritans' on the phone
Because whenever in the avoidance of isolation you want assistance

Lots of different charities and social clubs can help you cover oh quite a distance

viii. Be Happy Forever, Sad Hardly Again Ever

Sadness and worry gets you nowhere at all
Just drives you up the wall
Instead you should think positively forever
Seeing things negatively again never

You should never let illness
Bring you to any stillness
But continue to fight on
Until your problems are gone

In this world everyone does achieve a great lot
Though think positively they do not
Where-as if you think 'I Am Very Happy' as your endeavour
Alone and with others you'll smile forever

So remember 'Never Give In'
For that's committing a sin
Just treat yourself to many a smile
And you'll be cheerful for oh quite a while

© Paul Wilkins 11/07/08

ix. How Are People Thinking Healthwise?

Having a Personal, own problem I guess
Brings many peoples normal life to total stillness
They have many a thought and feeling of strain
That totally gets on top of them time and time again

Via true care and understanding shown by a loyal friend
Most of this would come quite comfortably to an end
Whilst circumstances having given it a 'title' or a 'name'
Makes it re-occur in the sufferers mind time and time again

If you wonder what could be quite a disturbing name
It is Doctor, used time and again
Or people with a relationship title such as Father and Mother
Being used time and again rather than any other

If you wonder what I mean by an in-descriptive title being wrongly used
I mean such as just Mental, Epilepsy, Diabetes, making people confused
Other than Professionals giving people's problem an un-explicit name
Health Consultants should always say 'Health problem called…' time and time again

Rather than the silly name such as 'Doctor' said to you and me
'Health Consultant a much more natural name especially would be
Rather than Mental, Epilepsy, or Diabetes etc. just being used
Health problem called… is a much more natural title to all the time be used

© Paul Wilkins 21/08/08

11

2. An Introduction to Psychological Exercises

Here in this chapter you will find a few clearly explained relaxing psychological exercises I've developed, thought out, and had lots of people feeling much better through.

A few other deeply psychologically experienced people who've looked at these, given them a careful thought and judgement, have called me a genius in putting them together.

The following exercises are all different ways of controlling your thoughts, by getting more stuck on your mind what you would positively like to be thinking, and more fully off your mind anything you'd like to completely put behind you, and never think of again.

Just follow the instructions carefully and precisely as instructed and you'll soon be feeling a lot better.

No longer a regretter.

If you'd like more of my psychological knowledge feel free to visit website www.emotion.poetryemotion.org.uk

© Paul Wilkins

3. How I Got to Control My Own 'Thoughts'

For years I had had all sorts of psychological/thought problems, but when in hospital suffering some stress via lots of confusion at work, and socially, a coincidental event or so where to take place to help me get better in a different way to Health treatment and medication.

I one day alone in a room had just finished on a sheet of paper writing out a positive affirmation of a sentence, when I was made to without thinking – just automatically – slam my book shut, in a panic, when I was distracted by hearing the room I had been alone in door open – someone coming in.

Just after slamming my book shut, and easing off from being made to jump, I noticed the affirmation of a sentence come automatically back to my mind again – without me needing to look where I'd wrote it again.

Having this taken place, I thought 'Oh it looks like that affirmation is now secure in my mind' 'It might go to my subconscious/back of my mind if I don't for a while look at it wrote in my book, which would bring it to the front of my mind again?'

Later on in the day I noticed my affirmation was still able to be recalled by me quite easily, still stuck on my mind, which I thought was a good sign.

Thinking about how with this affirmation stuck on my mind I would have a thought to ease off with whenever I had too much trouble in other areas on my mind, I twigged the most intelligent fact I'd had for quite a while, which was:-

- I was not to tell anyone else what my personally made up and secured in my mind positive affirmation was;

- If I did each time it came to my mind it would be distracted by the thought 'Like I told.............';

- If you excuse me I'm not going to tell you here and now what my positive affirmation - now positive thought stuck in the back of my mind/subconscious - is either, or each time it comes to my mind in the future it will be distracted by the sentence 'Like I wrote/typed up in my explanation/publication of discovering it'.

I think every personal thought counts/has a large effect on what I'm like.

i. A Psychological Exercise – "Have A Check"

ii. See This Article (Dr. Dolittle)

iii. How To Get Troubles And Upsets Off Your Mind

iv. What Is Causing Weddings

v. Teeth Consultant

vi. Some Healing Of Love

vii. No Need To Worry

© Paul Wilkins 05/04/2009

i. A Psychological Exercise To Help Get Troubles 'OFF' People's Minds

Through lots of different mental health problems I've had, but searched for lots of tremendous answers to, all to be seen on the 'Emotion' Section of website index www.poetryemotion.org.uk here about to be revealed is one of the most amazing ones. One in which via careful verbal communication, and no pen or paper needed, people can help/assist one another in very easily getting health problems or events 'OFF' their Mind for good'

As said in the title here are a few instructions on how to help people get troublesome thoughts/events 'OFF' their Mind:-

Exercise:-

1) Ask your friend to think of and speak out any event or health problem they'd like to get 'OFF' their Mind.

2) In reply to what they say just say 'Yes' or 'OK' and your friend will have that event or health problem 'OFF' their Mind for good.

Alternatively if it's you yourself who'd like help in getting something completely 'OFF' your Mind I'd recommend you getting one of your close friends to go through this exercise with you.

© Paul Wilkins 07/05/2015

ii. Doctor Do Little

The thing in the whole world that is getting everyone world –wide worse health-wise day after day, especially, though not only, people with psychological/behaviour/Mental problems is the inexplicit unnatural title 'DOCTOR' being used day after day.

To give evidence of this I'd like you to put yourself in the following 2 situations:-

1) One day you are at home feeling very stressed, upset, depressed, lonely, mentally upset not knowing what to do. A friend of yours by chance is walking down your street and by chance when passing your house thought 'Oh I haven't see such and such for a while, I'll nip and see how he/she is getting on'. This friend comes knocking on your door, coming not to your personal expectation, asking how you are? GIVING YOU THE CHANCE TO NATURALLY SPEAK OUT AND GET OFF YOUR MIND WHAT YOUR PERSONAL PSYCHOLOGICAL PROBLEMS HAVE BEEN – THANKS TO SOMEONE CONTACTING YOU AND ASKING, NOT YOU HAVING TO THINK ABOUT CONTACTING SOMEONE TO DO SO

2) On another day you are again at home feeling very stressed, upset, depressed, lonely, mentally upset not knowing what to do. With no-one contacting you for ages to help you naturally share your problems, get them off your mind, you're getting so upset you feel that you need to do something before you get even worse. The only option you have is to ring up and make a normal/or if necessary emergency appointment to see a person with an inexplicit title of Doctor, AND BY YOURSELF MAKE UNNATURAL PLANS OF WHAT TO SAY TO HIM OR HER WITH A 'TITLE' EXPLICITLY MEANING WHAT?

Which of the above two situations would you prefer to be in? If you haven't guessed already, most people I've put in these situations so far have opted to Situation 1.

One way to make psychological Situation 1 more applicable to people, without having to send people to their house when they're not expected, is to change the SILLY UNEXPLICIT TITLE 'DOCTOR' to something more NATURALLY THOUGHT EXPLICT such as 'HEALTH CONSULTANT', 'HEALTH ADVISER' , 'HEALTH ASSISTANT' etc

With a reference to a 'HEALTH CONSULTANT' I'll think NATURALLY about going to see them for a 'CONSULTATION ABOUT MY HEALTH'.

With a reference to a 'HEALTH ADVISER' I'll think NATURALLY about going to see them for some 'ADVICE ABOUT MY HEALTH'.

With a reference to a 'HEALTH ASSISTANT' I'll think NATURALLY about going to see them for some 'ASSISTANCE WITH MY HEALTH'.

WITH REFERENCE TO A 'DOCTOR' I CAN THINK OF THIS WORD EXPLICITLY/NATURALLY SAYING WHAT?

OR IS IT AN UNEXPLICIT/UNNATURAL CONFUSING 'TITLE'? BRINGING HEALTH PROBLEMS FORWARD MORE!

For an important petition/video about this please visit website

www.poetryemotion.org.uk

© Paul Wilkins

iii. How to get troubles and upsets Off Your Mind!

If you're having difficulty/feeling down, via any particular word or name, here for you is a minor psychological technique of getting it Off Your Mind, making you a lot more at ease.

Exercise:-
With a felt pen (Not biro) write down on a piece of paper the word or name you'd most like to get Off Your Mind.

Put this piece of paper in a bowl you've filled with water

By leaving this for up to an hour or two (looking at it every so often) the water will dissolve via the piece of paper gradually removing what you've wrote with a felt pen on it; and therefore, from the moment the word or name is totally removed, get it fully off your mind.

I wish you best of luck in getting problems off your mind.
To get lots of different health problems Off Your Mind I'd recommend you getting the unnatural/unexplicit word 'Doctor' Off Your Mind, using this technique too. Because as I've put in another article on this website this word staying stuck on people's minds makes all 'Health Problems', mentioned to one of these, uncomfortably thought of a lot more often.

© Paul Wilkins 02/03/2013

iv. What Is Causing Weddings/Marriages Not To Last?

I believe I have the answer to the above question

With 2 further questions I can reveal what I have figured out being done wrongly

Wedding/Marriage-wise at this moment in time, as it has for ages, building up the divorce rate.

Isn't it said, always been said, that the best way to get something off the mind, out of your system is TO WRITE THINGS DOWN?

WHAT ARE THE BRIDE AND BRIDE-GROOM ASKED TO DO EACH TIME AT THEIR WEDDING OTHER THAN 'SIGN THEIR WEDDING CERTIFICATE', 'SIGN AGREEMENT SLIPS'?

VIA DOING THE JUST ABOVE MENTIONED, THEY'RE TO SOME EXTENT LOSING THEIR EMOTIONS/LOVE FOR EACH OTHER.

It would be a better idea for relations/parents/the best man to sign the wedding/marriage certificate rather than the bride and bride-groom.

Alternatively if there are agreement sheets the Bride and Bride-groom HAVE TO sign themselves, individually, they should always end 'ON BEHALF OF MY BRIDE AND I, I AGREE.....' AND 'ON BEHALF OF MY BRIDE-GROOM AND I, I AGREE.....'

NOT JUST 'I AGREE ....'

© Paul Wilkins 01/11/2008

P.S. To get 'Much Closer' to your partner, having had a Marriage, I recommend getting 'Wedding Certificate' Off your mind using the Psychology article titled 'How To Get Troubles And Upsets Off Your Mind'.

v. Teeth Consultant

While you may have seen the point I've given, clearly, a few times about the Unnatural/Unexplict word 'Doctor' staying more stuck on people's minds making health problems thought of more therefore suffered more, and the need for it to be changed to a much more Natural/Explicit title which staying a lot less stuck on people's minds would make health problems thought of a lot less therefore suffered a lot less; I now have another similar point to make.

Especially for people having lots of trouble with their teeth/jaw could it prove helpful in getting this off their mind to some extent by changing the Unnatural/Unexplicit word 'Dentist' to a much more Natural/Explicit title such as 'Teeth Consultant' which staying less stuck on people's minds would result in trouble with their teeth/jaw noticed a lot less.

This is no-where near as important as the word 'Doctor' being changed but maybe something at a later no rush date to be considered.

© Paul Wilkins 04/04/2016

20

vi. <u>Some Healing Of Love</u>

```
H E A D      B O D Y      N E C K      A R M S      H A N D S      L E G S      F E E T
E X N E      E H E E      I X O I      L O A T      E N I E U      O X O T      I X X H
A T D F      S   F S      C T M N      L U G Y      A D C F P      V T O A      N T C E
L R I I      T   I        E R F D      N N L        L   E I R      E R D N      E R E S
T E N N      N            E O          D I E        T     N E      L E   D        E L E
H M I I      I            M R          F            H     I M      Y M              M L
Y E T T      T            E T          I            Y     T E      E       R        E E
  L E E      E            A            C                  E                 D      L N
  Y L L      L            B            E                  L                        Y T
    Y Y      Y            L            N                  Y
                          E            T
```

© Paul Wilkins 13/05/2018

vii. No Need To Worry

Here is a brief explanation of a big mistake lots of us make 'thought-wise':-

Lots of the time, when people, young or old, ask themselves thought-wise if they'll be able to do something? And the one word answer 'NO' comes to their mind, they panic over what's coming to their mind, and whilst trying to ignore the rest of the thought message/sentence get upset.

Where-as if they'd let the thought fully come out rather than it just saying 'NO' and that you can't do something, it would most probably have come out with something a lot more positive like 'NO Need TO Worry, You're Going To Do Fine'.

So whenever you're getting a thought message wait until it's FULLY come out before concluding whether it's going to be a negative or positive one.

a. HAPPINESS

I have love, joy and delight
Each day and night

I am thinking positive forever
Be sad again never

What I'm forever after
Is the joy of laughter

I am providing a smile
For oh quite a while

I feel enjoyment today
That is here to stay

I am happy forever
Be upset again never

22

I now have the most joy
Since, as a kid, I played with my first toy

I believe in myself
And can find perfect happiness and health

I take things as they come
Stay up with my thumb

b. HEALTH

My eyes water with delight
Now I'm free from fright

I regularly play and watch sport
Just like I ought

I never smoke
Don't want to choke

Having my perfect health
Is worth much more than wealth

I've gone from weakness to strength
At a great length .

I've climbed many a mountain
And watched my troubles fall from the fountain

I never let illness, bring me to stillness
If I were to die, many people would cry

I am as fit as a fiddle
And that isn't just a riddle

c. LOVE

I now have a wife
Who brightens up my life

Or

I now have a husband who's kind
And that I truly find

I can get away from hell
And in life do very well

I can to heaven find my way
On this and every day

We all show each other love
As much as Lord God above

I am showing a very warm heart
And in giving love play a part

I have some good self-esteem
Or so it deeply does seem

Each summer in the sun
I have plenty of fun

I am popular forever
Be lonely again never

I have plenty of romance
A love, kiss and dance

d. WEALTH

I now confidence have found
To always be around

I intend to continue to succeed
No matter how hard a deed

I am having a financial success
No more in a mess

I am getting a very good job
To earn quite a few bob

I am having a successful career
To drink to with beer

Prosperity is coming my way
With no delay

I take work, one step at a time
And never decline

I don't ever descend
But know I'll get there in the end

© Paul Wilkins 27/08/2018

4. Summarisation/Conclusion

By now, you should have benefitted from Paul's creative thinking, which will have influenced your thought cells enabling you to see life from a more positive angle. Where there is loss there is gain, and you should see the positive side of both the loss and gain. Paul will have shown you how to make constructive use of the unfortunate things in life which happen to us all combining them with your experiences and mistakes and turning them into positive factors. You should now feel more in control of your feelings and be less threatened by external negativities.

5. Closing

Hi to all you people after more Happiness and Success –
Like this book can provide.

I've always been creative minded. When at school I was
good at art and craft.

Over the last two decades I've been developing more and
more creative writing/creative thinking

In this book I'm sharing lots of therapeutic poetry and
quite decent Psychological exercises.

I hope you enjoy reading it, and have deep success in
getting much more positive/happy through it.

Paul Wilkins

Paul was born in Preston in 1968

He's half Welsh via his mother being born in Bangor,
North Wales, and knows that area quite well through
constant trips there.

His interests include art, playing badminton regularly, and all round creative writing/thinking.

He has over the last 2 decades done more and more poems, hymns/carols, lyrics, affirmations and jokes (bringing the medicine of laughter) despite having none of this when at school.

He lives near Preston (Lancs) where he's had a career in the Civil Service but now has many other ambitions to work on.

www.poetryemotion.org.uk

Printed in Great Britain
by Amazon